three
hearts
stitched

poems about adoption

three
hearts
stitched

poems about adoption

celaine charles

EGRET LAKE BOOKS
SEATTLE

Egret Lake Books
www.egretlakebooks.com

Library of Congress Control Number: 2024930115

978-1-956498-08-0 ISBN (paperback)
978-1-956498-09-7 ISBN (epub)

First Edition
1 2 3 4 6 7 8 9 10

To the parents who made me, so that my true parents could bring me home and make me whole.

contents

birth mother

adoptive parents

child

birth mother

confusion

(Birth Mother)

I wonder if
I
can possibly
possibly
care for you
as I should.

I wonder if
you
will ever
ever
love me
as you would

her.

(Adoptive Mother)

I wonder if
I
can possibly
possibly
care for you
as I should.

I wonder if
you
will ever
ever
love me
as you will

her.

heartbreak

Three hearts that day,
a sonatina…though we know how it ends,
how love is knit into pairs.

Sun and Moon
wrapped their arms around
their souls, suspended in time.

Only a glimpse
where all three entwined, all three
joined in a dance.

Only a nursery rhyme
to keep time, to keep rhythm
for a day or so.

According to the law
while clocks ticked, fermata…bid ominous,
and hearts slipped.

But we know this melody, the last verse
hums in heartbreak
for just one.

blue skies

She soars through blue skies,
mother bird,
though gray clouds lie snug against the day,
though rain threatens her horizon,
she flies onward with the wind,
away from the day's judgement.

Moon rises in the dusk,
a gleaming hint of sunlight,
like a lantern lit
behind thoughts in her mind,
past decisions made in fear
of the looming night

evermore blue in her memory.

heavy heart

A gift,
a blessing,
a moment unforgiving.

Accident,
mistake,
a chance of near escape.

Nine months
on loan,
payment due in grief.

One heart,
two souls
tempo in a dance.

Spared life
celebrates
heavy heart—a second chance.

among the reeds

I could not be the one to set you free
in a basket among the reeds.

Your noble father bore the task,
while morning sun sat behind

a cloud, its own rays afraid to witness
the sadness of the law.

And I joined him, concealed behind
the shade. The gloom that would be my sail

guiding my journey. I felt the wind
kick up its heels, astonished with the rules

there could be only one. Only one
when your time came to be. When you

came to be…unfortunate. And in fear, your father
took you to the village market. A note

in your hand. If ever you feel lost, or
without…whenever a cloud crosses the sky

and cloaks the sun, then you should know
I've wept for you, I will weep for you still, I will
ride

my river of tears into our next life
where I will find you once more,

the sun on your face. Then I will hold you
in my arms, freely among the reeds.

your wings

I will set sail to you,
and free your wings.
I will put you adrift
until the stars align
one day,

in another world,
at another time.
This won't be our last
encounter, not
with faith like fire.

Our bond is resilient,
and destined
for tomorrows, so
I am not sad today,
as you're lifted from my arms.

Those weren't tears you felt
on your cheeks. They did not run
like rivers to the corners
of your eyes,
sunken mirrors to mine,

reflections of hope—
for your constellation,
a sign for me.

Though we won't meet again
for some time, I'll stand,

my gaze on the sky
at water's edge,
to catch glimpse of you,
your wings
ascending to mine.

blinking red and blue

Lights swirl,
like confetti on a stary night.
I wanted to make you a birthday cake,
vanilla with rainbow sprinkles…
but the pull of my nightmare
was strong.
And my arms,
weak.

You grew heavier and heavier,
even in your tiny shell.

Now my dreams blend
unnaturally with reality.
Silver bracelets clasp
over bony wrists,
moonlight my only witness,
and you are gone
you are gone
you are…

Gone are the days of dreams,
and birthday cakes,
and star-filled nights
like the one when you were born.

Gone is the trust in love,

that it was enough.
And those decisions
I made outside myself,
have come to collect
in their haunting.

So now, gone
is my freedom.

And you are gone too...
in a swirl of lights
blinking red and blue.

delivered

Beautiful infant
safely delivered,

innocent soul
devoured by choice,

vibrancy
cries in the night,

cherished
alone
alive.

wait

I love
You
Need to
Wait
Just one more time
Just one more
Hit
Me again
In the face
Knock me out
Let me
Try again
Fresh new
Start
Third trimester
I can do it
Next
Time
It will be okay
I swear it
I swear
If you take my baby
Away
He
Goes
To new arms
Reaching

Tentacles
Seeking my will
Power
Strangled
With substance
Abuse
Your soul
My new
Crux
Filled
With more
Than love
For
You

my greatest mistake

My error in judgement wasn't that night
because I chose that November moment
between the sand-buried cattails and picket fence.

I rolled out the patchwork quilt from Gran,
though she'd have turned in her grave had she
seen the tub of fries and cans of beer set out
between us. Surely she'd have blushed had she
heard the smack of my lips on his, the rip
of my skirt zipper not quite swallowed up
by the swells of the gulf behind us.

Music played from his car radio, but I can't
remember the song because his breath was in
my ear, along with the waves and kisses, but
his hands on my heart stilled me. And I wanted
him. I wanted him. I wanted—

He left after that. I replayed the moment over
and over in my head, though I told no one, until
I discovered his Valentine, tucked deeply away
in my soul. I stood on the sand that day, winter
blowing my hair, but there was no sound.

Maybe
my greatest mistake was saying nothing on that
shore. I was too quiet and too young and too

something far less daring than the pounding waves.
I just wasn't ready when you were. I needed to

grow, at least that's what I tell myself every
November when I lay out Gran's patchwork
quilt across the white sands and cut pink paper
hearts to hide under shells and bury along the shore
behind the cattails waving hello.

Maybe you'll find one. Maybe my littered heartstrings
will be the crumbs we need to reunite—because I'm
braver than I was back then, more courageous than
the seagulls swiping french fries from my hand, and
the wind wiping the beach clean—clean—clean.

My greatest mistake wasn't that night.

never meant to be

It was never an option to terminate
this baby, rolling
within the confines
of my belly.
It was never to be
forgotten, or lost
on the wind
behind tears
and time.

When that phone number,
s c r a w l e d
across the phonebook,
g l e a m e d
in morning's light, like
a shooting star, I knew
this baby was never
meant to be
mine.

relinquishing rights

The concept of giving up a child is
not for the faint of heart.
Such final decisions fuse
against our sense of self, our desired ability to
forget and move on when knowing
something
of our own flesh and blood
is out there, in the world…
to realize
it might be safer
to never mention such stain
on our souls…

One never speaks of giving up
their parental rights—
These stories fall on judgmental ears.
The tales show us
as the antagonist
in our own life's story. But
sometimes the villain has a story too.
Sometimes the villain
can be a blessing, when
relinquishing rights
was the choice that
saved you.

how many babies

This baby is the third child,
I mean fifth child,
I mean ninth child—unwanted
pregnancy—I've carried.
Maybe I wanted them all
secretly
in my heart.
Sometimes when I'm alone
at night,
or in the early stretches of dawn,
while the world still sleeps,
I hold my belly and dream
of a different girl
growing up,
in a different world,
where my mother protects me
from the dangers of
oppression and fear,
pain and guilt,
and the lowly acceptance
of who I am—which
in the eyes
of everyone around me—
I am nothing.
I am unworthy.
I am undeserving.
I am an animal in a cage.

And when they feed me,
I eat.
And so, this new baby
that I carry
once again,
can simply slip away
with the rising sun—
For I am awake now;
my dream is done.

i am not a monster

I don't want you
right now.
But I don't want
you
not to be…

So,
please understand,
down the road,
when you wonder about your past,
when you wonder about me,
If you do
wonder
about me…

I am not a monster
I am *not* a monster
I am not a *monster*

I just
couldn't be the person
you needed me
to be.

they say

Now, with time gone by,
they say
it was a gift,
that I set you free,
because
I couldn't care for you.
I was too young.
Because I was too...
something other than everything I was.

I was in love with you,
though it happened by chance.
It doesn't expunge swollen emotions,
nine-months longing to meet you.
My aspirations and dreams to kiss your head,
to cradle my pinky in your grasp,
to hold you when you cry,
to tell you I will never leave you and somehow,
some way,
we would manage just fine.

But they sent me away
to a safe place,
they say...
Safe from myself, I suppose, because I was made
to feel shame,
to feel remorse for my actions

by wrongly creating you.
Suddenly, I was an abomination
to be extinguished,
or at the very least
hidden away
from the damage I'd become…

They say.

sadness

I can't say your name anymore,
not that I did before,
out loud.
But always, it was there on my tongue,
soft and warm, like a mama bird.
I tucked you in
and swallowed you whole, for safe keeping,

my baby bird.

ache

Will it ever be gone?

This constant ache
between the bite of my teeth…
or is it comfort now?
My jaw forever clenched,
your essence pinned to mine,
sharp needle and thread.

Endless pressure pulsates
in the back of my mouth,
throbs along with
each swallow of air,
as if I gave you my last breath
all those years ago.

my greatest achievement

He is the single greatest achievement of my life—
the baby boy I carried for you.
The baby boy I loved *first*,
for you.
At every moment, he was always *meant* to be
yours.

three hearts stitched | 37

dear baby

I know you won't remember me—awake
living your new life somewhere—away,
but I hope we can meet in your dreams.

I will be the one waving from afar,
a green scarf in my branches.

I will be the cool tingle on your toes,
the rain that pulls you from sleep,

the honey goodness in your hair,
warm and secure in the questions
I know may find you.
So, seek me only in rest

because glorious mornings will bloom
and I have new roots to plant
a little later, down the road.

It rains here and there, but when I awaken
there is forgiveness to sow and reap and
bake in my bread, its fragrance
the most delicious of truths
from my past—

memories with
and without you.

my say

There's no such thing as a free lunch.
That's the first and last thing I learned in economics.

Someone is affected,
or put out,
or a sacrifice is made
somewhere, at some link in the chain.

Choices are the same.
Any choice made
bears weight,
and at the very least
restricts
any freedom to which
one thinks they have rights.

Rights to stay.
Rights to go.
Rights to judge.
And every choice
carries
a life sentence,

for you,
and...

the soul created,

the others involved,
whether they choose or not.
This freedom is all encompassing.
It has no
boundaries,

and even
that winter's day,
such freedom
didn't seem to hear
my voice,

my say.

birth mother

A bundle of benevolence
spread, even with rough edges.
Goodwill, lightly dusted
with a dose of truism.

Judgement acknowledged,
sour on the tongue, though
sweet to the patrons, an
unspoken, cultural
juxtaposition.

The world loves a giver,
they devour the prize,
though once it's done, we
ought not speak, the
ordeal, one-sidedly
private.

Yet you extend niceties
in return for
false hopes,
shameful self-loathing,
ridiculously so,
because at least you
smiled and bowed in.

tumbleweed

August morning
cuts
through overcast skies.
Sharp edges lack
shine, though reflective
just the same.

Cold, geometric shapes
sit stoic
in a room,
square
window to the sea,
for a secret, unseen.

Rectangular bed,
solid,
to bear the weight.
Sheets tucked tight,
with triangle corners,
flags in surrender.

Parallel lines, folded flat,
atop blanket and pillow,
objects meant
for comfort,
lack means to merit
such condolences.

Cold room, circle lights
illuminate
a small sphere
of life, free
from its seed pod,
no longer round, but flat

against a bloody sheet,
the same one intended
to soothe.
Though once free,
this tiny thing,
vulnerable

with potential,
blows away in a breeze,
unknown, unheard,
untouched, now
tumbleweed
in a world left

with only hope—
asymmetrical
rays to light
a new way,
treasured gift—
your journey begins.

time's letter

Time drops in now and then like
a long-lost letter. Correspondence
from the past. A moment spilled in
ink. Its razor-sharp reminder signed
to the page. No exclamation points
needed. Just one essential signature
separated me from you. My past

forgotten for a spell, until the wind
blows. Nature's delivery service through
rain and shine. Never a missed opportunity
to relive the day I decided…*they*…
decided. A choice was made and upon
delivery, like a letter sliding between
cold metal slots—I mean unopened arms—

you were on your way. There were no
takebacks. My fingers couldn't pry
the steel lock. The arms of uniformed
nurses—I mean postal employees—carried
my bundle far away. Stamped and delivered
with no return address, unless you count the
winds of time, caught within the empty mailbox.

h o p e

*H*ardly a day goes by I don't think of you.

*O*pen flowers in bloom nearly all year long.

*P*oppies, cyclamen, aster, and iris,

*E*nough reminders to never forget.

adoptive parents

my prison

Wedged between tight spaces,
between decisions with no ground,
my feet can't even float
above my head, because
I am caught,

pinned between absolutes,
so, I exist…like
the stone that traps me,
smooth on the outside, and I smile,
lest they see my loss.

While inside, my heart,
rough and jagged,
grows cold in my thoughts.
Possibilities cling,
like rain to roots,

for the freedom I covet.
A phenomenon needing charms
and prayers, surreal mysteries as
I place my hands on both sides
of my prison and breathe…

to the unnatural beat of time.

these words

She changed her mind.
She
changed her mind.
But, she changed
her mind.

Every time I say these words,
the feelings spill out
with inflection
in different places,
and they all strike

at my heart,
in my brain,
at my side, keeping me keeled over
on my closet floor,
dilapidated.

a gift

Without pretty paper,
silver bones and golden hair,
shining regal delivery delays
gratification.

Beyond blue boxes,
stacked high to the heavens,
an altar of luxury, unwanted
for exchange.

Outside lengthy surprise,
expectation, desire,
we wait and wait for time
gone awry

Ignoring the questions,
and comments that chide,
soulless, half full
felicitations.

Until a morning, surreal
after many slow seasons,
to one long night,
YOU

arrive
with the sun.

answered prayer

Who decides this miracle?
God's time
is not my time.
Even when I prayed,
as I should…
I went to church.
I tithed, though never enough,
I know.
But, He knows
my heart,
and the expense of it all,
He must,
because I've paid in tears,
on loan,
and pushed
empty carriages
down lonely aisles.
And time,
sweet time ripens
far too fast
for my desires,
my longings…
when I've done
everything right,
everything
I could possibly do…
waiting and waiting

with empty hands,
and wrenched heart
dripping
all that I am
on the stone floor
of my garden—
without *you*.
Until
that
moment

He decided.

tiny one

Wind carries seeds across the field,
a breezy dance to fix
the upsets in nature.

Golden sun cradles dripping dew,
leaves caress the cheeks
of summer, chapped and ready

for cooler weather. All the while,
time staggers, hidden from view,
pausing to wait,

wait,
wait.

Time tells—it always knows
when seedlings find their way
home, finally, unexpectedly—

like lupines pierce
a rocky ledge, or
dandelions rise amid
gravel rocks.

We know the world is set right

when a tiny one with petal lips
rocks in the arms
of a stranger.

haiku: five words about adoption

Terror

She might change her mind
What if she changes her mind
What if she doesn't

Elation

Exhilaration
In the impossible coup
My baby is home

Gratitude

Angelic heartstrings
Woven starlight delivered
Bestowed miracle

Uncertainty

Sunrise turns to day
All ten fingers and ten toes
Reach for their future

Blessing

Oh baby of mine
Mirrored eyes claim my forever
Secure in my arms

goodbye, baby girl

She wipes joy
from baby girl's cheeks,
her eyes closed tight
as puddles run,
rivulets over
mountaintops.

Baby girl tries to sleep
unaware the tears
aren't hers to shed.
She's been here before
on these battlegrounds,
armored in vulnerability.

She's walked these floors
at night, both hands
on her lower back,
burden in her belly,
heart burning
the scorn of loss.

Nausea coats her throat,
but she'll volunteer
again and again, offering
the crook of her arm
for the unwanted
she can't have.

One last time,
she bends
over baby girl.
Birthmother
changed her mind.
She whispers blessings,

carries her tiny vessel
onward to deliver.
No need to look back,
the moment forever
marked in tear stains
over mountaintops.

bundled gift

Bundled gift delivered
as if by storks, as if
a favor traded deep within
a childhood forest,
enchanted story, fairytale
told, tale after tale after
long awaiting, light
glimmered a new start.

Rumpelstiltskin slept,
his name whispered
on repeat, repeat, repeat,
as if a lullaby sung, as if
a star-wish born, soared
from the dark night of my
womb to the bright measure
of your heartbeats,

prancing rcindeer gift,
warm skin, tiny fingers
reached, as if petals
stretched for the sun,
as if *you*
were always
meant for *me,*
bundled gift.

dear new baby

I've waited for your arrival,
weeks and months and years
of procedures and losses,
of dandelion wishes and rabbit-foot
hopes buried deep, under multiple
mounds of sorrow.

But now you are home. My heart
once crushed to ashen fault
transforms, renews in swirls
of astound. Angels sing,
a new dawn breaks…
my empty womb is full.

will you ever know?

How will you ever know
you are the pebble in my
shoe on a long walk
beside a rocky shore…

Will you ever realize
you are the pea beneath
my mattress, a tiny ping
against my spine…

reminding me always
and forever that you
are mine to bear and hold
and love—and love—

and love—at the same
time, you are forever
never mine. At least the world
reminds me it's so, but

you should know, I would
choose this journey again
and again—the pain, the
loss, the waiting—all of it

just to call you mine!
I will wear these shoes.
I will trade my sleep…
to walk alongside you.

j o y

Just when I believed I was meant for no other...

Our phone rang like church bells, announcing miracles.

You are now forever...all ours.

already loved

The paperwork matters not
because we already love you.

We already see your edges blur
with your sisters and brothers,

and with every new member
of this family you've never met,

but surely will come to know;
you are already loved.

always navigating

This family and that family…
songs from birth and stories
about adoption. What's real?
What's imagined or made up?

How much to divulge? What
to hold back…until the time
is right? When will that time
be? Will the truth cause trauma

or indifference or lifelong pain?
How to navigate the questions…
shambolic, and so I squash them all
into a ball, wind my throwing arm,

and hurl every unknown or God
forbid, the knowns we wish we
did not know into an abyss,
awaiting sound and reassuring

songs and stories to remain
about this family and that family,
about adoption, and what's real—
always navigating what's real.

new seedling

Is it too soon to scoop you up?
Your baby seat…the only innocence
in the room…sits by a metal office chair.

Nearby plants are fake, dust-filled leaves
no longer green, like the spark of you
spilling from your bundled essence. Your

onesie is used, as are your first minutes
and hours and days of existence, but
we are here to renew…to recreate and

grow colorful blossoms, reap fresh memories
to replace any dormant trauma from
behind your sleeping eyes. Oh, my wee

precious seedling, together let us scatter your
dreams and wishes along a new path, grow
ourselves into a lovely garden once you wake.

But for now, I fold my hands into my lap, for
fear I'll scoop you up and plant you in fresh soil,
water and watch you bloom before the paperwork

is even signed.

plans

The reality of Adoption:
It is traumatic.
New parents may not have been the plan,
at least the first one. Adopted babies have
a longer journey sometimes. Their travels may
find forks in the road, with bends and curves that
take their breath away, leave them nauseous and
motion-sick. Foster parents often pray for the
reunification of their borrowed children, through
tears and sorrow, believing there must be a bigger
plan. There must be…though sometimes…these

little souls simply need another fresh start, another
journey to begin anew. And even though it may
not be the first plan, it surely becomes the most
beautiful
next step in the infinite scheme of things.

birth announcement

A tiny bud soaks in dew,
rainbow kissed from angels,
dancing in morning's first light.

Soft petals seek golden hands,
to bathe them clean, to dress
their crinkled folds with warmth.

Wriggled stems straighten under blue
skies, ivory ribboned condensation,
green wings and flushed cheeks.

Birds herald the news, your birth—
announced and presented—without
care of laws, or choices, or people.

Your birth, accepted into being,
marked by the pines and reveled
by the dancing sea, forever perfect.

already there

We flew to her because she was there
for us, already waiting in a world
where she was wrong. Where she was thrown
away for being…who she was.

We flew to her because it was right.
Why create another soul, adding more
to a world already full
with so many others…right there.

We flew to her because it was wrong
not to go, not to consider her
as our own rightfully chosen
child, waiting patiently…for the world to decide.

songbird

The wonder is real,
finally
it exists, and I chime at the top of my lungs
like a songbird.

The ballad begins,
though the verse
has played in my mind for some time.
Time measured

in heartache
until now
you are mine, asleep in my arms.
Every minute

of waiting
gone from my memory,
nine months extended to…
too long ago.

And so, I sing,
joyful I didn't break in the wait,
in the quiet unspeakable white noise
for you.

forever family

What makes a forever family lies
in the wake of every day.
My little one peers up with hands
for holding, clinging, and never

letting go. What makes a forever family
is in the waves of adolescence
as hurtful cries "You're not my mom—"
crash against heart-shores, cause

erosion's sting to fall in silt and sand,
though with time, soften to spire-
-topped turrets, encircled by the
deepest moat; a stronghold protecting

this forever family—repairing the
long-ago wounds, bandaging strain
with everyday scrapes and cuts along
the fierce winds filled journey.

This forever family will stand—
on jagged cliffs, gazing over the sea,
swaying our flags for all to see, and
declare, "We will always be

 your forever family."

mothers are

Mothers are women who birth their young.
They are women who raise babes,
born from other wombs.
They are women who give their babies
away
to another mother's arms, either by
choice or persuasion.
Mothers make difficult decisions,
no one can judge.

Mothers are men who decide to stay,
with feet like roots, they raise
their own babes.
Mothers are men who care for their young,
who tend to the needs of
children
who might not be their own,
but they stay—
they stay.

Mothers are community
who grow gardens.
They seek to plant and feed,
to sow seeds of culture and
guidance—that may or may not
come from home.
Mothers are community

because they spend the most time
with our young.

The world is filled with mothers
who need mothering themselves…
mothering from
women and men and community,
mothering from
people
regardless of blood. People
regardless of baggage, or intention. People
regardless of mood, or expectation, or reciprocation.

Mothering comes from the sky,
independent of storms and weather.
Impartial of forests or land
both
undiscovered and trampled through.
Mothering comes from the earth's
bountiful belly,
birthing a world in need of
mothering.

Mothers are the earth.

child

wanted, unwanted

Wanted, yet unwanted—
a tiny silver thread,
translucent like a raindrop
or a tear.
The world, clearly
distorted and

stitched through
time and years of
shimmering fabrics,
colors twisted and bent
in the light, collected
at the hem.

A cloak once worn
in the afternoon chill
until the sun rose
and the garment
was cast aside,
unwanted, yet wanted.

nine months

Part 1: Mother

In the nine months
of uncertainty, now certain,
you are gone.

And I am left here,
cradled arms still clinging
to the last weeks and months

you rolled and kicked. A composition
of tiny heartbeats thrumming
in the mix of pouring rain.

Part 2: Baby

In the nine months
of uncertainty, now certain,
you are gone.

I heard you lament
within the walls of my cocoon,
a ballad of sorrow—

yet also beauty, regret,
and then a euphony of hope—
even now, between paper bibs

and hopeful smiles. I am
held by many arms, rocked
in a harmony of fresh rainfall.

baby girl

Baby girl lost
or
baby girl left.

Maybe baby girl black for my hair,
or baby girl blue for my eyes.

But only baby
to her,
for she never knew.

And always
I wonder
my baby girl name
for those thirty-one days,
alone.

three days old

I can't put her down.
If I do, I can't stop looking.
Her tiny nose
budded
in rosy cheeks.
Long black eyelashes
tucked
in folds of shiny silk,
hidden
mirrors
of mystery,
but I know those eyes...
And they know me.

They   know   me.

I weep in pure joy
at this tiny bundle.
My anchor to the earth.
My blood in her veins.
Something all mine, only

three   days   old.

Then, once again,
in those early moments
of my own

made-up memories
from my own, faraway birth,

three   days   old.

And I lay hushed
in my crib,
no need for tears. Just more
space than before,
more room to stretch my soul,
to float away
and disconnect...
from the snug
warm
tight
inside

her burden,
her fear,
only...

three   days   old.

for the angels

Angels were there that morning,
in the quiet solitude of your decision.
The bittersweet choice I should thank you for,
because I have words to speak
and tears to shed.

In the slowness of that summer heat,
you must have suffered.
You must have felt bitter,
or lost, or sad, at least
part of me hopes it's true.

I felt it, you know, that
delicate kiss imprinting my soul.
Maybe it was you.
I like to think it's true sometimes,
stretching tales to fall asleep.

But I know you closed your eyes that day,
as did I with cries unheard,
and hunger neglected,
my comfort, a hospital crib
to hold such tiny bones.

Please don't cry for me,
enough sorrow spread
in the light through my window,
the one facing the sea...

yet still, there was good.

I felt the downy plumes
left on my pillow.
I felt their warmth across my cheek.
I still wonder sometimes, it was you
who left them there, and I should

thank you, but for the Angels, instead.

i saw the light

Star gazers found me
long before,
when light broke through
the lingering night of my
beginning.

Peering up from my landing spot,
watchers came and went,
eyes changed color, shifting
like the various arms
that held me.

They had much to say
in each embrace, though
few words came with
morning sun, or
moonlit nights.

I suckled my fist, or finger
offered in response to my
calls. Each heartbeat
reciprocated in adoration,
sympathy, judgement…

But when I was alone
in my cradle by the
window, and the room
was still and quiet,
I saw the light.

when you're abandoned

He's not a baby,
he's a man.
Older than a boy, at least.

He was adopted then,
so, he can handle
himself alone.

It's innate,
when you're abandoned.
You don't even feel it

any more
or less than
what's expected.

His father thought he was fine.
His mother thought he was fine,
to be on his own.

Any future mistakes
made outside the
contract are only

legally binding
when they're babies…
It's when they grow up.

It's when they grow up.

gravitational pull

Waves ebb and flow against the shore,
against the years I've grown, tied to
an endless, gravitational pull.

Some mornings, downy white sands
soften my senses, my wonder,
and I am content with the sea.

Ocean winds once carried me, wrapped me
like a blanket to swaddle, unnamed
womb, shelter from the chill.

Other nights, surf sprays against my cheek,
pink and chaffed from dreams, where
mermaid songs tempt and tease…

Don't forget she left you in the wake,
remember you were unwanted,
miracle of life, abandoncd.

But the tide rolls in again, pulsing
in step with the moon,
lies revealed with ivory froth.

You are a treasure, buried
by the ones who gave you life,
found by the ones who gave you life.

stubborn and strong

My mother smiled,
or rather smirked
to the world,
at one time telling her
she would never hold
her desire.

And instead
my mother,
stubborn and strong
said,
"I don't care,"
and did it anyway.

And she did,
any
way.

She picked me up
and held me close,
while my father decided
I looked like him.
And I did.

Then my sister came,
most naturally,
and for my mother,

stubborn and strong,
everything fit
in the world,

because she smiled
and made it so.

the mix of us

Her ultimate sacrifice became our miracle,
and I don't quite have all the words
to adequately say how I feel,
to show you my true gratitude.

I wonder…does my sister,
fully yours, ponder in her thoughts
about appreciation and pride,
about relaying to you her thankfulness for life.

I don't know if her burden is as heavy,
though not to compare. That thread
you stitched between us, neatly,
respected, the only difference in our eyes.

Thankfully, you never cared from where
I came. You only threw me into the mix
of us…our great togetherness,
from her ultimate gift.

thumbprint faces

I see faces like thumbprints,
each and every one
unique
with possibility
to be mine.

Spring blooms in my garden,
familiar by names,
hyacinth
and marigold,
though each petal remarkable
in its own truth,
and shape.

At times
one stands out
as more beautiful
or interesting,
a peacock in a hen house
strutting its heritage.

Could it be mine?

blood in my veins

More than blood runs through my veins,
more than heritage or heartfelt stories
about how my great, great, great
grandmother traveled
across the Atlantic Ocean
three times in her long life,
packing flower painted bowls
snugly wrapped in her luggage,
each trip.

More than blood runs through my veins,
more than photo albums
filled with family faces
that never really looked like me,
but I imagined that someone,
in the background, might be
my long lost
somebody
I might one day meet.

More than blood runs through my veins,
I've longed to belong to someone
somewhere
who shares that same
blood in my veins,
wears my gaze, and laughs out loud
at the curly cue feathers on duck bums.

And then, I look up
at the *someone* already there.

More than blood runs through my veins,
my heart stomps out a new beat,
clutching faded memories, string-tied
to the chest of someone
holding porcelain floral bowls
who bore someone
who raised another someone
who wanted someone
like me.

to be happy

Can I be happy
when others are sad?
Can I sleep soundly
while others stir,
nightmares holding
hands, gripping souls…

There is unrest in
the world today, much
abuse and neglect and
forgottenness and death—
yet you found me—me.
Can I not feel fortunate?

That you were there that
day, one month later, thirty-
one days before they planned
to send me away. Can I not
feel luckily and gratefully

thankful for your precise
timing. For choosing me. For
providing me the chance
to be happy?

beauty in a broken heart

"You were wanted
and picked out,
I promise."

Proving words alone
cannot mend
a broken heart.

I know you love me,
yet there's no need
to internalize
my loss.

You had the power
and saved me,
only,
you can't take on
her sacrifice
or burden, or
mistake…we'll never know.

But one thing I know,
years of
"I love you,"
was surely enough.

Irises bloomed

along borders
of a hole
always there.

Weeping willows
shaded my
angst
for most years.

And you should know
how tall I *still* stand,
even with that void
notched in my side...

Broken heart still beautiful
because of you.

dear birth mom

I never think of you. Not
when I grew up nestled
in evergreens, far from the sea.
Cradled in branches, away
from the rushing roar of sorrow
scratching the coastline. Sun healed
my wounds that day. It was not
until I grew old—enough to notice
the abscission of my leaves. My
hues shining a scant unlike theirs,
though they never minded. I was
genuinely loved, you see, so
I never needed to think about
you. Only here and there, when
a wind rushed me sideways,
caught in a gale, those little
dirt devils pause for no one,
uncaring when one is already
far from their roots, far away
from the sea. Sometimes
I think of you.

maple in december

A new year soon,
though I stand still,
frozen beneath layers
of frigid sentiments,
hidden deep beneath
furrowed rows of rind,
concealing flesh.

I am not all I appear to be.
I am more than the seed
planted long ago. Years
upon years weathered
my shape, pulled me
toward the light, formed
my shade, soft now against
snow-covered grounds.

I move more in the spring,
playful with the wind—
by all those put in care
of me. Blue sky with her
cherished mate, the sun, and
my dear friend, rain. How I
treasure visits from beetle, though
he hides from lullabying birds
until winter falls.

Such beauty, though, snow,
even when sorrow travels
in tow. Silence chimes like
stilled bells, and I long
for my companions to return,
to tell the story of my birth,
all those years ago.
My seedling dreams
remember
another from
another time,

another soul who cared
for the earth above my head,
who chased away
beetle and bird,
who forced my roots
to weave wide and
broadly stake
my ground
until I grew
stronger,
taller—
so tall

I could not see the earth below,
there was no need.
My branches sway long now,
dance in the breeze
high above the hill line—
awaiting a new year.

my father

My father wasn't my father,
but my father he became…

Like a sunset melting sky
bleeding over mountain top
with violet hands grasping,
and apricot eyes glaring,
challenging Night to pry
his fingers from
the hope
he had

in me.

everything's okay

It is not okay

I felt welcome in my own home.

Though sometimes I was a stranger.

These outsiders brought me in.

Among these hearts who love me.

They said, "You are ours, and we are yours."

At times I felt...disconnected.

But they meant it. They have always meant it.

Even if I didn't always feel it the same way.

You look like your father, they would say. It was sort of true.

Me—getting too inside of me—feeling too outside of them.

Our trifling story sparkled with glints of sapphire.

I always wanted my dad's eyes...bluest on a summer day.

And I wore dishtowels on my head, feigning long hair of course.

Always wanting everything I wasn't.

I wanted the auburn locks from my mother's past, long gone.

Always finding ways to be different.

She wears her hair short now, and it's gray like her journey

I can't explain the walls I built and tore down again and again.

But her voyage carried her to me...or was it me to her?

None of it mattered because they only opened their arms wider.

And now, every day is okay.

Everything was always okay.

forgotten father

Forgotten father
snagged between the pages,
memories of mother and child while
words trickle like the creek behind Grandma's
house, buttercups like periods and exclamation
points, the story ends there. The end. The end
has never had a chance to begin, too many unknowns,
the wonderings of *what if.* What if he never knew
a baby to be? What if shadows were all he left behind?
What if the pain was too great for him or her or them
to stay? What if he only donated this piece of himself
for a cause? One greater than himself?
What if he wanted the baby but had
no voice…or choice? What if I tug
on this snag? What if I write
a new page?

set free

I love you.

I love you   to the mother who raised me.

I love you   to the father who called me his own.

I love you   to the mother and father who left me—shared me—chose a new path for me.

I love you even if you didn't love me, or the world oppressed you with their rules at the time.

I love you because even in joyful delight or unrighteous sorrow...

I was set free.

have you ever thought about finding your birth parents?

I am often asked this question from strangers who know their heritage.

Never have I been asked by someone adopted themselves.

Maybe it's the idea that I wouldn't need to,

since *they* know

and I don't...

but, *no*

I don't want to know...

except sometimes when I do.

Sometimes I wonder about things—things like the sound of my birth mother's laugh,

or the laugh lines creased in my birth father's smile when he once looked at her. What made them laugh? What made them smile?

Or did they?

I can only hope they liked each other, at least for a moment. I hate to think of the other reasons I may have been put up for adoption.

The reasons I don't like to say—even think about—
though the thoughts are there.

Force—such an ugly word to think sealed my fate.

One night stand—such a petty way to find my way
into this world.

Worse—the idea that I was *any* kind of mistake.
And more than that, if the mistake belonged to
someone other than my parents.

I've read books of women long ago, shamed, their
babies stripped from their bodies and given away
as if a better choice.

For who?

If my parents wanted this choice—then I see it as
a gift. But if they didn't—I don't think I want to
know. I would rather think for a lifetime—I have
always been wanted,

surely meant to be from a higher power—*yes* that's
what I believe.

So, *no*. I don't want to know.

Except when I do.

in love once

My mother loved my father once...
a full cup of sweet, southern,
sun-on-the-beach
love.
I am sure of it.

My father adored my mother,
the way her skin shone bronze
under frothy gulf waves—
love.
It must be true.

Lost in their embraces,
footprints in the sand until
impulsively, they sailed away…
in a happily ever after kind of
love…it must be.

At least, I imagine it that way,
as the alternative brings sorrow
and regret and emotions I
simply don't want to feel.
So…

My mother loved my father once,
and he loved her, too.
There is a reason for everything,
even when love sails far away.
I am sure of it.

ireland

Ireland is the land of my past,
the land of rolling hills and coastal
shores, washing over the bones
of my ancestors.

Buried secrets beneath hushed
voices and faery rings, awaiting
claim, though I have
no name.

It was given away, whispered
to the stars, tossed in the sea
green with envy and lust to be
someone.

To be the roots of a sessile oak,
grounded secure with legends
and heritage, a kinship to call
my own.

But alas, I was alone, left in a cradle
of waves and wonder. Adopted
into the universe…and…then…
loved.

rejection

Rejection is real,
even when you're told
you are chosen,
you are wanted,
you are loved.
And still somehow
there's a little snag
on the bottom
left side
of your heart,
a loose thread
jostled
by the slightest
movement,
barely a brush
or a breeze
scratching gently,
as if not to harm,
only a reminder
in case you
forget.

she's portuguese and i'm adopted

"She's Portuguese and I'm Adopted."
I recited at a young age,
amidst joyful faces
and hidden chuckles.

It was the fortitude of my childhood.
A masterpiece in the making,
painted in broad strokes
for permanence.

Blue skies
and my daddy fixing
anything broken,
even bones, and then
my heart.

Mama worked as a nurse
and picked berries
for canning.
Daddy fixing,
Mama mixing.

Summers were colored with "You're fine," or
"Time for bed," and always
"I love you,"
with strawberry jam.

Winter wonderlands fell during the night,
but only footprints in the backyard,
or on mountain tops,
bundled up,
and cocoa from the thermos.

This was my life,
never distinguished
borders dividing.
"You look like your dad" they'd say.
Heritage woven thick.

reminders

Beach glass,
sharp edges
worn smooth.
Piercing
abandonment
flux
with age.
At dawn
souls renew,
remembering
who they are,
while sand
dissolves
beneath toes,
gripping
in tide's pull.
Waves crash,
tossing
comforts from
moments ago
to sea,
to thrash
against rocks,
reminders of
loneliness.
Longing
for arms,

unfound,
until dusk
takes hold.
Tides rise,
filling gaps
in the sand,
tiny grains
with mountain
strength,
reminders of
familiar
butterfly kisses
and cocoa
on the beach,
chilly at
sunset,
tangerine fingers
reaching,
turning chins.
Reminders of
today.
Reminders of
tomorrow.
Reminders of
every soul
holding ground,
edges softened
with age.
And with
the tide,

hearts flare
as winds toss
green and blue
sea glass
until settled
on sandy shores,
battered
and beautiful.

love

There are no words to describe
my full heart,
pumping like fire,

raging like the creek
from my childhood, where
Dad took us camping.

The bluest lake you've ever seen,
as perfect as Heaven,
I imagine.

Mom sectioned the makings for
S'mores in Tupperware containers,
enough for each night.

Sunshine rained
like miracles that summer
I learned to waterski.

I don't know how he did it,
but Dad turned
my terror upside down.

I learned to fly, an unbeliever,
until his miraculous faith
pulled me up from the water.

Then, he winked at me,
and that was that,
my heart was full.

That moment,
that wink,
my pride burst its seams.

Though today, my heart breached
once more, surpassing its borders,
spilling over,

pulling me above the surface,
water's edge like stained glass,
when slowly,

like the creek emptied
mountain snow in my childhood lake,
you slid into my arms,

and Heaven winked—
I swear it.

dear mom and dad

Thank you for choosing me.
And thank you for continuing to choose me
every day after that.
Thank you for the years
of stability, while others have naught.
Thank you for the experiences you
assured that I had, no matter how afraid
I might have been…
learning to ride a bike,
learning to swim,
learning to be independent and on my own.
I was always afraid of leaving you,
but you were—are—always there for me.
Thank you for being my mom and dad.

author's note

Adoption is a triangle—connecting the birth mother, child, and parents who adopt. Every experience is unique for each individual. I am only one adoptee…who tugged on a thread.

Today I am overjoyed to share this collection of personal poems about adoption, including some fictional pieces inspired by true stories I've found in my journey.

I've always known I was adopted, even before I knew what the word meant (see my poem, "I'm Adopted, She's Portuguese"). My parents engrained in me how special it was to be chosen, and I need not feel anything beyond that…even if at times I felt otherwise.

And that ideal alone seeded this collection. Children who are adopted may feel completely loved and completely alone all at the same time. And that's okay.

I experienced a happy childhood and am grateful to my family for treating me as their whole child. Not all adopted children have this experience. Many adoptions are open now, meaning the three families know each other. My adoption was closed, meaning all documents were sealed. Yet in both cases, there are always questions…many unanswered questions.

I suppose my poems came from this place. Never knowing my heritage, I wrote poetry to find answers. Never knowing how my birth parents met, I made up stories. Never understanding why I was given away—well, you can see where curiosity has taken me. My heart goes out to every human involved in the corners of adoption...the birth mother and her sacrifice, the innocent child caught in the middle, and the parents adopting...including the ones who foster.

My poems cannot possibly cover the gamut of all adoption stories, but I've included a few belonging to me, even some reimagined and embellished. My purpose is to open the conversation about the multi-faceted experiences of adoption. I hope you enjoy...and please consider supporting a local foster and/or adoption organization in your community.

With love,

Celaine Charles

acknowledgments

Thank you to the many souls I spoke with over the years, sharing adoption stories and giving me permission to interpret and transform their thoughts into poetry of my own. I want to extend enormous gratitude to T.G., L.M., and the two T.M.'s, among others…you know who you are. I am grateful for your conversations and for becoming the inspiration to grow this book beyond my adoption story. I hope all humans touched by adoption can stay stitched together and know…you are here for a reason. You matter. You belong.

about the author

Celaine Charles is a teacher by day and author by night. She's an award-winning, multi-genre writer who balances her dual life creating poetry, fantasy, and blogging about her journey alongside students, family, and friends. How does she manage? Walks through the enchanting forests of Washington State, reading fifteen minutes a day, and mounds of allergy-free chocolate help this creator thrive.

FOLLOW THE AUTHOR
www.celainecharlesauthor.com
instagram/cc_celainecharles

about egret lake books

We are a small, independent publisher.
If you like this book please leave a review on the
platform where you purchased it.

FOLLOW FOR MORE BOOKS
www.EgretLakeBooks.com

www.ingramcontent.com/pod-product-compliance
Lightning Source LLC
LaVergne TN
LVHW051556080426
835510LV00020B/2999